Fresh Ink VI

An Anthology of Poems

authorHOUSE®

AuthorHouse™
1663 Liberty Drive
Bloomington, IN 47403
www.authorhouse.com
Phone: 1-800-839-8640

First published by AuthorHouse 09/29/2011

ISBN: 978-1-4520-5633-3 (sc)

Printed in the United States of America

Cover design by Robin Michel
Cover art (Benthos, etching) by Chantal Guillemin
Contact us: freshink6@yahoo.com

Fresh Ink VI
An Anthology of Poems

Rita Flores Bogaert

Jannie Dresser

Chantal Guillemin

Constance Hester

Madeline Lacques-Aranda

Ellen Levin

Robin Michel

Adam David Miller

Mary Milton

Barbara Minton

Charles E. Polly

Sue Prince

Joon Stoddart

Julian Waller

David White

Fresh Ink VI
An Anthology of Poems

PREFACE

In 1991, sparked by the desire to write poems and improve those in progress, we formed a poetry writing group and called it Fresh Ink. We started out as students of poet Jannie Dresser and have met twice a month in members' homes to get our poetry fix, share writing exercises and news about poetry happenings in the Bay Area, eat snacks and enjoy each other's company.

Over the years members have come and gone, and some of the original group still remains. Others have moved away but have been impelled to establish Fresh Ink satellites in their new homes because the group and the format fill their need for poetry, the reading, writing and improvement of it. In this anthology you will find writing by current and former members, as well as poetry by our inspired and inspiring Jannie Dresser, who continues to touch base with us from time to time.

When you read our biographic statements you will see evidence of the writing games we play: some of us have used the results of an exercise based on *Smith Magazine's* six-word memoirs instead of the traditional bios.

Rita Flores Bogaert
When I was a cup of tea

When I was a cup of tea
I was a very good sip
a very good sip for the woman who took out her blue bone china
      sat on her red wingback chair
      gave herself to the luxury of quiet
      in her white linen dress

When I was a picture window
I was a very good view
a very good view for the little boy who watched tall branches
      the bluebirds perched there and
      the squirrels that shook off its nest

When I was a pair of socks
I was very good wool
very good wool knitted by a grandmother blind at seventy
      who loved radio stories
      she measured her grandson's foot by one length of her hand

When I was a red carpet on tile floor
I was a bright rectangle
a bright rectangle that defined the room
      within my confines I heard his proposal
      saw the diamond ring and
      caught her dropped shawl

When I was the purple leaves on the plum
I was a very good shade
In autumn after I shed leaves
      the stick shadows of my limbs stood witness to the hole dug
      There she will lay
            best friend of the little boy
            who watched the bluebirds

Rita Flores Bogaert
The Color Red for Papa Isidro

This is what I know about Papa Isidro:
He listens well
I cry about my shrunken retirement account
He tells me about the sure return of the bull market
"Save your money, keep saving," he said.
He knows I need reassurance.

He does not like clothing in the color black
Around him, wear happy bright colors,
all the colors of the rainbow
colors of the prism, colors of daylight
No darkness at waking hours, I admire that!

He loves sharing good food
In the Philippines,
at Seaside in Macapagal, at Aling Tonyas
he feeds me fresh catch from the sea
Creatures, alive just before its plunge into heat:
squirting mussels, crawling crabs, slowly squirming shrimps
We eat these together and sweet orange innards of crabs
He nods and smiles
I see my pleasure is also his

I walk out of Aling Tonyas
With this feeling:
Papa Isidro's generosity feeds me
In partaking, he becomes part of me
Shrimp, mussels and crabs I will digest into proteins
Amino acids will cruise my bloodstream
My heart will beat into a song
love/love, love/love, love/love
My blood's color is in the rainbow

Rita Flores Bogaert

In another life,
I was your guitar

You toiled 'til the torrid sun traveled
across and over the trees along the skinny river
then, you ran home from the fields
along the harsh and coarse lanes
between rows of sugar canes.

You took me down
from the highest shelf
where you hid me
safe from dog and children.

You cradled me gently,
dusted and polished me
inch by inch
'til my shine and smoothness
pleased you, then you played me.

Slowly, you strummed my strings.
Your hardened fingers slid
up and down along notes
on my long fretted neck
while warm winds fluted the husk
in the emerald field.
You hummed a melody-
thrilled at ending a day
of hacking sugar canes.

Finally, you chose a flat pick
and plucked and strummed
and my sound box vibrated
with the music of the wind
and the trill of the maynah
that hovered over the fields.

Rita Flores Bogaert
Cantaloupe Soup after School in Fourth Grade

My mouth yearns for cold and sweet and wet on very hot days. At the last school bell, I think of the large jar of cold cantaloupe soup—its glass sides beaded with condensation. In late afternoons, the vendor woman scrapes melons down to the green of the rind into long strings of orange fruit flesh, saves all drips of melon juice from the pulp into a large jar then adds sugar and water to make soup. Minutes before school is out, she drops ice into the jar. After our short stroll under umbrella shade, I buy a big cup of this cold soup at the fruit market in Remedios Street near our school. My best friend, Arsenia, buys a stick of fried bananas coated with streaks of melted sugar and hot just out of the oil. We walk to Manila Bay, sharing small sips of the cold soup, pushing strings of fruit into our mouths with a straw and take turns blowing the burn out of the bananas. We snack as we pass along shops selling lacquered bamboo chimes adorned with seashells. Arsenia clucks those dangling display, reaching a hand up, while humming *la, la, la, la, la, la* as she tips the stick of banana for me to take. We giggle louder when shopowners give us a frown. We arrive on the bayshore, our belly full of warm banana but saving just a bit of the cold soup. There we put on shorts under our skirts, then strip out of our school uniforms and shoes. We stuff our clothes into our school bags. In our undershirts and shorts, we wade to the water's edge, slowly soaking wetness, feeling slimy mud between our toes. Arsenia often splashes me first, smacking water on my tummy. After a few splatters, my sweat washes off. We play and laugh for only a few minutes, and then return to the last sips of sweet juice and eat strings of cantaloupe settled in the bottom of the cup. Then we both walk home.

Jannie Dresser

Once in a While

I am a car whose brakes have failed;
No stopping this backward slide
Into black night splayed by rain.

I am the empty wine bottle,
And the shriveled old man
Who smiles in the corner, smacking his lips.

I am the hurdy-gurdy and the monkey
Who dances at the foot
Of a pier, too smart for words

And the trickle of water heard
After the classroom goes silent,
The teacher's voice fades.

I am all sight and illusion,
Tricks of the mind, a wallop
In the stomach on a Saturday night,

The Tasmanian devil feeding
On a wallaby struck by a jeep:
Night-steeped foliage my joy.

Jannie Dresser

Lessons from the Sufis

When you give up ruling the world
you find your lover sucked out in a whirlpool, you find a friend facing
up to a gunman,
you find yourself on the sidelines making notes, smiling at the brave.
On the way to Jerusalem many dangers:
sand storms, thieves, children
with hungry sockets for eyes.
Still there is one thing you have lost;
having lost it, you know you can
return. The Holy City in disrepair
ready to receive you. Don't you know:
life is that whirlpool, that gunman
denting your cheek with his black pistol, who goes "Boom." And
there you are, staring
into an opened umbrella, the man like a spray of salt sea air
dissipating in the wind and
just beyond the police line, you catch sight of a crowd of people
holding yellow balloons,
laughing furiously.

Chantal Guillemin

Garden Spectators

Garden spectators, watch the drama
Anchored to earth by long, slender necks
Comment in the breeze to each other,
Listen and laugh from sandy beds.

Curious, they watch the three-belled tabby
Stalk deaf, careless swallowtails
Who revisit the familiar anise
Where, as caterpillars, they once dwelled.

Did they see, under cover of dark
From the pear tree, two bucks boldly snatch
Tender, young, green leaves near the bark,
And leave the petioles still attached?

Silent witnesses, in late summer
Eye birds in flight and those at rest
Reel from the handle of a metal pail
And, upside down, sip some cool water.

Onlookers, lazy and somnolent
With heads that bob and shudder and tack
They're the globose leek flowers
That wait for the next garden act.

Chantal Guillemin
Dandelion Seeds

In a white and woolly wardrobe
Wandering, weightless and windborne
Over weeds and watsonia
Waft the seeds of dandelia.

Launched by wind or curiosity
Tiny, grey umbels in a flurry
Burst and scatter in disarray.

Then, without word or warning
At the whim of a whirlpuff,
Soar wildly skywards
And vanish in a wind huff.

In a while, in perfect balance
Some sail by with nonchalance
Only to be whipped again
By the next williwaw.

Chantal Guillemin
Phacelia

Phacelia, flower of bees,
With leaves, lacy and lobed
Upon hillsides and prairies,
You grow near the gilia globe.

Uncoil your mauve arabesques
In graceful, scrolling fronds.
Your petals emit wild scents
To lure pollinators near and 'yond.

Furry fingers in a mudra hand
Extend from blood red stalks
That rise from the untilled land
Over ancient paths and faults.

Hoarded seeds from your withered claws
Guarded by brittle, spectral stems,
Escape and hide 'til the rains of fall
Surprise, soak and soften them.

Phacelia, flower of bees,
With leaves, lacy and lobed
Upon hillsides and prairies,
You grow near the gilia globe.

Chantal Guillemin
Ode to a Garden Beauty

to Reynaldo

Such vegetal beauty, such grace,
I could gaze upon thee an hour,
Admire thy dimpled, pallid face,
Call thee 'my sweet cauliflower'.

Bewitching is thy moonface glow,
On me a spell has truly cast.
Thine light within shines like a globe.
How long can this enchantment last?

Curious aphids with thoughts of evil
Could damage Nature's perfection.
It would take but just one weevil
To mar my lovely creation!

With veil of leaves, thy face I'll cover
From the wind, winged and the solar.
I'll take a peek, just like a lover
And kiss the dear fruit of my labor.

When soon my sweet will be the size
To steam and serve, I will excise…
Let us not mention the act, no, never
When with a knife thy head I'll sever.

But until then, I'll be thy valet
And free thy bed of London rocket,
Ensure thy curd is never smudged
By sooty mold or other scourge.

I dream of, dread, the day that we
Will unite in final harmony
With butter, cream sauce or vinaigrette,
I'll commune with my sweet coquette.

Constance Hester
Heaps to Sweep

I sweep the splintered shards into a dust pan.
Toss them into a large black hole, the rubbish
bin of memory. Long slivers, sharp and brittle,
occasionally surface long after they have been tossed,
still cut as bloodily as the broken dawn.

In the distance I hear the cries of a workman,
pounding, pounding, trying to force a piece
of swollen wood into place. Another sharp sliver
surfaces, you cried out that way in our love making.

The ground is damp from Southwest monsoon
rain but soon it will dry into a powdery dust
and even rocks won't hold it down when the wind
blows. I'll let those brittle memory shards also blow
away with a puff of my breath.

Constance Hester
No More Love Sonnets

The earth smell of pinto beans set to boil,
a book of love sonnets by Pablo Neruda, waiting to be read.
A red-breasted house finch builds its nest in porch eaves.
Gray clouds menace east of the Sandias.

A book of love sonnets by Pablo Neruda, waiting to be read.
I don't write love sonnets, too old to be drowned in love.
Gray clouds menace east of the Sandias,
clouds gray as my hair, grow rosy in setting sun.

I don't write love sonnets, too old to be drowned in love,
passion is for the next generation.
Clouds gray as my hair grow rosy in setting sun.
Sun kisses the clouds, but kisses are denied me.

Passion is for the next generation but
I don't cry for myself, love has wrestled with me.
Sun kisses the clouds but kisses are denied me.
I don't mind because memories tease and tickle.

I don't cry for myself, love has wrestled with me.
The earth smell of pinto beans set to boil
are part of memories that tease and tickle.
A red-breasted house finch builds its nest in porch eaves.

Constance Hester
Return Home (to North Carolina)

It is the land that speaks to me:
the green mown fields, the stands
of pine with Lake Hickory, Catawba River

edging the woods and fields.
They were there when I was born,
there when the people whose headstones

in the cemeteries at Newton, Taylorsville,
Moravian Falls were born. At night
the moon shines over those pines, lights

mown fields. In the afternoon storms
of lightning and thunder electrify
the sky, send bursts of rain to keep

fields green and pines springy. I smell
the grass, the pines, the wild honeysuckle,
feel content to be in the place of my birth.

There has always been something here
that calls to me no matter where I am living.
Sometimes in dreams, sometimes at the sight

of a magnolia tree or the feathery blooms
of an acacia in some other state. I have deep
roots in this place. Now and then I must

come here and drink deeply
before I can once again roam
and love
the roaming.

Constance Hester
You Slut!

Drifting along in Foley's Department Store
on the morning of my 66th birthday, I noticed
that pink in shades from bunny to brick
was the hot color this year; pink Christmas trees,
pink panties, pink luggage.

From out of the store's ethers came a whimsical
notion, it would be fun to buy a slutty pink shirt,
a skimpy shirt – knit, tight, with lace showing
at the bosom and at the hem. A slutty little pink
shirt like the teenagers were wearing. I could feel
the giggles rising in my throat.

I spotted a slutty pink shirt with black lace
that was just the thing. And on sale! Five dollars
off! I bought it (on credit), brought it home.
I could hardly wait to try it. Put on my tight denims,
pulled the slutty pink shirt over my head, looked
eagerly in the mirror. I fell out laughing. Where
was the teenager I had envisioned myself to be?

She was nowhere in evidence. In the mirror with one
hip cocked was a woman too plump, too wrinkled,
too old to be wearing a slutty pink shirt. I quickly
pulled it over my head and pushed it into the shopping
bag. I've simply got to quit taking that teenage girl,
the one that hangs out in my memory, to department
stores with me. It's her fault that I buy slutty, sexy
clothes—and then have to take them back.

Madeline Lacques-Aranda
A Second Round of Irish Coffee

They've blotted the whipped cream
with a squirt
of glossy shamrock green.
I tap its summit with a skinny straw,
poke clean through
to the bottom
of the glass and twirl,
lobbing the glossy pile
against each rim
and back
until,
like a meadow's last hat of snow
it melts.

Let us drink, I shout, already drunk,

Let us drink
to the grey
muddy
grass
of spring!

Madeline Lacques-Aranda

Outside the Market

Rough
music, softly sung
revives their rough lives.

The blind singer
whose hand
on *corazon* ascends

from navel to heart,
as agave to blistered sky;
her song of gravel and fruit.

And again, her gasp of
Corazon
tumbles across barren gullies
onto lost roads of the listening night

as his husk-torn fingers
curve the neck
of manzanita carved guitar

its taut strings
of fishing line
threaded through crooked pine pegs.

His nails lightly rake down
a scorpion dance,
thrust off by rising thumb.

Torrential down strokes
flood the pain
but up up it comes again

picante pero sabroso

Madeline Lacques-Aranda
Teacher, What Means Target?

I draw a small red circle,
corralled by a series of larger black circles
rippling across the dry-erase board

I leap back a few steps and pose,
attempting to embody Orion,
the universal archer taking aim

I mime the release of tension,
the light arrow sprung from its mighty bow,
energy and intent aimed at the small red circle

Thwap! my muscles release:
Bull's-eye.
I turn back to face the class. Target.

Teacher, why make this for one store?
Store?
Oh, yes, *Target,* the *store.* Why indeed?

I turn back to the board,
and with green marker, surround the target with arrows,
all points aimed at the center.

Let's write the names of all the things
we want from this store along these arrows.

They come up one by one:
shampoo, pants, paper towels, toaster, socks, CDs, batteries.
Then another question:

Teacher, why you say is target?
To we is say Walmart.

Madeline Lacques-Aranda
Waiting for the 8:05

Beyond the hypnotic blur of highway traffic,
a quiet brood of hills waits patiently as hills will, to be noticed.

I scan loosely along their pelt grey horizon, and then peer closer,
where satin apple-greens tuck into a swath of mossy jades.

I see the crosses then.

I want to mistake them for a whitewashed Galician
fishing village, but my breath collapses fast in recognition.

How neatly they prick the slope, bloodlessly bandaged
among the wild blades of grass. They creep closer to me now,

like Macbeth's Birnam Wood. Five thousand lacquered stakes
lengthen and blush into flesh and wool, their stiff arms free

to hang at their sides, hands in pockets of jeans that sag
along the saddles of their hips, tall boys and fit girls

crowding the hill with their loose hugs and muddy dances,
muscles numb under the sweet weight of weed.

And every ribcage hums from the same rhythmic blast
of booming bass, each heart in its native place.

Madeline Lacques-Aranda

A Girl's View from the Pew

Somehow their souls transfigure
into worthiness every Sunday, these boys
who throw daily papers from their devil-boy bikes,
f-wording each other from mound to bat,
boys who cheat if they need to,

nasty boys who sometimes
fancy a feel of flesh beneath the nun's habit,
ordinary boys who wake in the same morning hour
as their sisters do but
get an extra biscuit and a ride to church.

Frocked in the toy vestments of God,
they enter the altar,
cowlicks sprayed tame, freckles scrubbed pink,
wearing shoes so shiny they seem to wink back up at them
as they genuflect.

With practiced gallantry,
they shake the bell for all to arise and bring water and wine
for the old man to bless and drink.
They glide the golden paddle beneath
the chins of churchgoers, ready to retrieve the holy disc
should it collide with a long tooth
or with lips that close a second too fast.

Their crude eyes survey the soft pink supplicant tongues
that arise from deep within
devout, sinful, ambivalent parishioners
invoking their paper savior
to melt his magic onto their lives.

When the last hymn is sung,
they snuff out the last flames of mass
with brass belled poles and exit through the aisle,
swinging scented ashes of sweet dry loss.

All rise and follow them out toward the light.

Ellen Levin
Penguin

She says of herself:
"I walk like a penguin."
her knee sore, swollen
from arthritis
Now in her elder years
she has one hip higher than the other
does her "penguin walk"
around her apartment
She goes out on the little balcony porch.
listens for birds.

She tells me she's wearing my father's light blue nightshirt.
feels he is holding her.
Sometimes I am touched
by things she says
When she goes to her psychiatrist she wears
a Monet flowered outfit
complete with straw hat and matching purse.
She offers a ride to someone lost.
I feel we are in a movie.

She has a clock that she ordered from a t.v. show.
It has a different bird song for every hour. When the hour
strikes
the bird sings
that is how she measures time

at the end of her life, in art class
with her teacher Victoria
she does a painting
she calls "Reaching"

wins a prize and is taken to an awards dinner
is very pleased
has received
some recognition   at last.

Ellen Levin

Hummingbird Wings

Dressed in my one beige cashmere sweater and pleated skirt, age seven
I look up at the dome of Eutaw Place Temple,
one of the oldest synagogues in the east
People were chanting "The Shema," a holy Jewish prayer.
I feel a yearning toward the spirit
If we can also know that sitting quiet
on a weathered wooden bench
is also a temple for the spirit
Being able to feel quiet
If we experience worry going away
Have a hummingbird come close
If we can remember
a few moments with one other being
If we know there are blessings in disguise
that things work themselves out
that stone and slate
have a way of changing shade
then the soul will find home.

Ellen Levin

Ode to beet soup

to Marian Yu

Maroon colored little bundle of joy soup

The color of raspberries
Beet soup made fuchsia by sour cream
Sweet as dessert

Grateful that a spoon
with little flowers
is magically right there

Cabbage and greens swim
in jeweled pink liquid
the richness satisfies

my tired soul

Ellen Levin

Once upon a time
Now… and forever
There was and is… a cat

a lump of warm fur resting next to me
she came into my life without my intention
she lived upstairs in the attic with her kittens
rescued by my roommates
she gave her kittens
plus an adoptee named Bean
all of her love
didn't ask for any herself
…except one day
lifted up her head for a pet under the chin

later in my room, waiting to be given away
after her kittens were gone,
she crawled under my covers
slept on my feet

It was then I knew she had come to me.
She reminded me of my friend Emily's cat, Nehama,
who I took care of for a short time
I had to give her away, always regretted it
I knew I had to keep Abbey
with her one half meows, like little bird chirps.

She is a great comfort to me
which is what the word
Nehama means in Hebrew.

My aunt's name was Emma which means whole or complete
It sounds like Nehama to me.
Maybe when one feels whole there is comfort.

Ellen Levin

Nothing Special

I've become quiet
from sitting in a chair
at Quaker Meeting
with others
around me

not pushing at me
not telling me what to think
from singing a love song to myself
"Daisy, Daisy
give me your answer true"

from watching the cat
the way she curls up like a snail shell
her quietness is like
the stillness
after the vacuum cleaner stops

she licks her paws
like that's all that really matters
her white socks like they just came
out of the washing machine
bleached and all

the triangle of white on her throat
the purring that seems to come
from under that triangle
when she lies down beside me just me
in my black and white prison shirt

covering my constricted heart

it opens
and begins to purr too.

Ellen Levin

Chanukah: light for my father

back east   celebrated lighting of the candles
with my father
                    sang Chanukah songs
helped him get dressed
so that he could   take his final journey.
My mother said:
"put his pajama bottoms under his pants."
            We found long under wear
A polar fleece vest covered his shoulders,
blue for his birthday   from Paul and Lorraine
couldn't decide on the hat,
a wool one with a brim or a rain hat.
We walked him in his wheelchair
down the long halls, where he lived   I wondered if he wanted to say
some kind of good-bye
He was small in his wheelchair
after being 6 feet

The walk felt too quick to me.
Was he ready to go to the hospice?
I wonder if he felt ready to go there?
Does anyone feel ready?

My mother said his Jewish Birthday
was the last day of Chanukah on the
Jewish Calendar.
He lived to be 91 and 9 days to the
beginning
of another Chanukah.

Robin Michel
Hairline Fractures

Running below the canopy of cottonwood trees
I marvel at the delicate beauty of the gold fan-
shaped leaves fluttering to the ground, the soft rustle
and sigh as they cluster together,
the various hues of gold turning white.

Yesterday morning's warm flush of October summer
had me thinking, *What is the rush? Just let things be.*
Today, I wake to frost upon the windshield of the rental car
and icicles as thin as hairline fractures upon the stiff grass.

You who were always so vain have let your hair turn white,
now walk with a cane, and in your own words,
"Couldn't care less if a handsome man is in the room."

The gold leaves slide beneath my feet.
One slip and I could fall, bruise my dignity,
or sustain a life-changing blow to the head.
I am reminded to proceed with caution.

One slip and you could fall: the back porch steps,
the tangled weave of your worn shag carpet,
unfamiliar dark corners, unseen cracks in the sidewalk.

One slip of my tongue, and all the work done to convince you
to return with me to my house 700 miles away could be undone.
You might choose to remain shut in your house
with its many dangers and no one but the cat, waiting—
while the branches of the cottonwood trees
lose their last leaves and stand bare in winter,
for a spring that may never again arrive.

Robin Michel

Feet and Hands

Your feet, slippered in worn tan moccasins
seeded with red and white beads, protrude from beneath
the large buttery robe and rest upon the hardwood floor
as lifeless and vulnerable as the discarded, crumpled tissues
you forgetfully leave around my house (your temporary shelter).

Your hands, poking out from the soft robe's
suddenly immense sleeves, shake violently, cannot be stilled,
no grace in their motion, no trace of ballet or jazz or hip hop rhythms,
only a spastic wail of trembling, independent of your will.

Your once restless feet that constantly practiced tap steps
beneath your parents' dinner table,
and later danced all night in clubs long after
others had stopped,
or paced the kitchen linoleum as you carried first one colicky baby
and then another, and another, and another

are now as still as the plastic Navajo Indian dolls
vying for space with the cheap trinkets
and garage sale treasures
littering the shelves of your beloved
and relinquished house.

Watching your hands shake, I remember how it felt to be eighteen
and to take your hands in mine before returning to school—
hands that overnight had grown smaller than my own
each of the tiny delicate bones beneath your skin
were as fragile and as tough as the ribs of songbirds.

Now in this hard moment of our lives
seeing your hands and your feet defenseless and small,
I forget (forgive) your long tongue and its black crowing shriek
unleashed as mean.

I want to hold your trembling bird hands to my breast
as if my mother's milk long dried up could feed and sustain you now.

I yearn to scoop up your tiny feet in my two hands
hold them to my lips, blow life into them, and watch you dance again.

Robin Michel
If You Should Die Before Me

Every poem is about love,
if you dig deep enough.

If you should die before me,
Saint Anne's pink light will cease to exist
and the City will no longer be my home.

If you should die before me,
I will cut my hair and join a convent,
polish wooden floors until they gleam,
and then polish them again.

You are a woman of words, you said,
and with those words you made me whole.
I need to get my mother, I said,
and you were the only one who knew it was true.

When I didn't believe in us,
you refused to not believe, too.

There will never be a very last love poem,
as I will retrace every step we have taken,
every word spoken, every moment we shared,
over and over and over again, until I can do it no more.

If you should die before me,
I will weep and weep and weep
an ocean full of tears and sail away
on a tiny yellow boat, in and out of all the poems
our love has created, until I find you once again.

If you should die before me,
I will carry my notebook to Kirby Cove
                    and I will write you back to life.

Robin Michel

To Do List

1. Water flowers on window sill.
2. First, buy pots, seeds, potting soil, hammer, nails, wood.
3. Build window sill.
4. Decide that a window sill needs a window; smash a hole in wall positioned directly above new window sill.
5. Crawl through window and make a new home in the branches of the orange tree. (unlike your friend's screaming son with Asperger's Syndrome, you love both the color and the fruit)
6. Ignore the stares and under-breath comments of the neighbors on your right, Jackie and Jerry, who already find you an objectionable neighbor.
7. While they sleep, using only the moon as a light, fill Jerry's shiny black military boots that he leaves outside their door with the potting soil and plant Peace Lilies.
8. Do not forget Jackie or how, before she stopped talking to you, she told you how she wanted to be another Esther Williams and had danced water ballet in the 1940s USO shows the same year her high school sweetheart Jerry was fighting for peace. Take one of your dead mother's glass mermaid figurines and wrap it up in the most delicate of seafoam blue tissue paper and attach a seaweed green bow of silk ribbons.
9. Climb back into the tree and keep on climbing higher, higher, higher . . . no windows, no ceilings no doors . . . the night air is fragrant with freedom.
10. Remember the song lyric you heard on morning radio: *God wants us to have the whole wide world.*

Now, you do.

Adam David Miller
Melon Slice Moon

Melon slice moon,
not yet enough to feed masses,
but wait.   This darkness
in the shadow will retreat
as she fattens, her flesh
fills our spaces.

Melon slice moon, once a sliver,
half-dark now.   What is
the miracle of your returning?
We know you will soon
swell with light.

Sliver moon turns to melon slice,
promise of sweetness returning,
you turn moon, we turn,
from darkness into darkness,
into light.

Adam David Miller
The Heart

After the mind goes, the heart stays,
tracking treasures no thought can conjure.
The beat of feet, light to my door
will bring songs soon. I can hear them.

Cornucopia heart, empty out
high notes, falsetto or true,
so we can snatch love sounds
now. Do. While there is still time
within this hour to shout.

Adam David Miller
Riding the Range of Thought

to J. Waller, M.D.

Will have to smash all thoughts before I can sleep.
One near coherent one will make my mind try
endlessly to tighten its meander.

Come back here. Can't be shootin' no chittlins
at no moon, leaping over no razor wire chasms,
climbing no squash yellow sky.

Let's bargain. Wait. If you permit me to grab
a few winks tonight, yes, just a few, I'll play scrabble
with you tomorrow, or solitaire. Name your game.

Smash *you* to smithereens? No, no nothing
like that. Here, take this chocolate-coated
lollipop. Sweet, sweet thought, just come
a little closer, just a little closer.

Adam David Miller
Planes of view

A

I built my house where I shouldn'ta
'Cause I couldn'ta built it nowhere else.
Now the flood done come and took it,
like they knew it would.

When they picked us up off of the roof,
me and my parrot, they made me leave
him behind.

Boat ain't no place, them people say,
For no squawkin' bird.

Henry was some good company,
the best I had.

B

We sent out two plane loads
to San Diego and San Francisco,
twin giant hollow birds jammed with
our dogs and cats. This while
bodies floated like bundles
bounding gently in the toxic gumbo,
and that one over in Algiers lay
soaking up sun and fetid air.

I helicoptered over the shifting scene.

These were folks I had seen
sitting on stoops, groups idling at corners,
never amounted to much. Oh,
those little ones, childr---

We even got out one parrot.
Ungrateful bird. Here we were
rescuing him, and all he could crack
was, "Goddamn your souls to hell!"

Adam David Miller
Sunday Visit to a Carolina Chain Gang

Nobody works on Sunday, we were a Christian nation,
we kept the Lord's day sacred, even here.

The men lay around, most chained to a low standing
bar that ran the length of the camp. Others sought shade
where they could find it, within

the watchful eye of the white man with a comfortable belly
and a double-barreled shotgun. Two bloodhounds slept
under a small tree on his right.

I played marbles with myself while my stepfather talked
with one of his buddies, to whom he'd brought some chicken,
rice and a slice of pound cake Mama made.

"Don't run off now," he shot over his
shoulder, as I chased my favorite taw
down a slight incline.

"Heard a man comin', comin' soon," his buddy said.
"Take most of these, I don't know where,
Georgia, 'labama, down that way.

Hear they got steel mills, factories an' like that.
Anybody got no job got to go. Had a job last week,
don't count. Got to have a white man say you
workin for him now, right now."

I spotted a boy not much older than I, lying
at the edge of shade as the sun moved,
he had stretched as far as his chains allowed.

I started over to him to see if he could play.
"Get back there!" the white man shouted,
the camp aroused, men stood, rattled their chains
the dogs alert, stiffened. My stepfather ran to me,
pulled me back to where we'd been.

"You better go, man. You know how
things get when Charlie revved up."

"Can't take you no place," my
stepfather chided, as he half dragged
me after him.

Adam David Miller
The Passing of Kan Edo

The cat killed and ate a curious rat,
crunching bones, savoring them but leaving
entrails, serving notice to all who listen
that none need apply.

Ants began to crawl over what was left of rat.
Hunger sated, the cat sat near the shoes,
looking up. Later the cat, after prowling
the empty cupboard, ran outside and set
up a yowl.

Next day the neighbors, missing Kan Edo,
found his body sitting by his bed.

Mary Milton
Miz Erin

"I cannot believe you gave her
my telephone number. And my cell.
No way I wanna talk to her.
Only thing I got in common with that woman
is that you pokin' us both.

"I think you got an alternative motive.
I think you trying to drive me crazy.
You wanna live with that woman
but you don't wanna give me a divorce.
I have always been a rationable person
but now you got me all discombobulated.

"You know, all the years we were married
I never, never disrespected you like she does.
She talk to you, she scold you like you a little boy
and you do whatever she want.
You one sorry excuse for a man."

Mary Milton
Upstairs, Downstairs

You live amid two bachelor uncles.

God lives in the attic
where he writes letters
to the editor and
to his elected representatives.
Sometimes he races down
in a cloud (he uses a lot of talcum powder)
to read his latest composition to you.

Satan lives in the basement
where he tends the heating system.
On his visits upstairs
he proves to be a charming raconteur
and mixes a mean mojito.
After he leaves, coins
and other small items go missing.

When you ask why they never married,
God frowns and proclaims that
he is too busy to look for the right woman.
Satan smiles and murmurs that
there are so many he cannot choose just one.

You don't want to be exactly
like either of your uncles
but you're glad they are in the family.

Mary Milton
Trading Spaces

The man working the cash register
is missing one finger and one-half.
He does not seem discomforted.
He gestures freely as he talks
with the customer ahead of me.

I want to rest his hand on my face
and ask how it happened,
was he frightened,
did he cry.
And I want to tell him

I have lost parts too
and have been scared
and that I think we all are
jigsaw puzzles
missing pieces.

But when my turn comes,
I simply give the man
some money and watch
his remaining fingers
make change.

Mary Milton
Kristina Adores

           bracelets
wears them over sleeves
wrist to elbow
chains and bangles
silver beads charms
dozens and dozens
           dazzle

Kristina adores
      her arms
scores her story there
Carved slices
fill with red
like a pen's ink
Private runes
      control

Kristina adores
      her dog
His warm wet
tongue licks the red
When she brings out
the blade
he wags and whimpers
          pleasures

Mary Milton
Rapunzel

noun — the act of letting down or letting go
verb — to let down or let go

It happens in sleep, sometimes in fatigue.
For orgasm, a requisite.

Your hands can no longer hold a weapon.
Your face, like flowers, turns to sun.

Rapunzel is a slow jazz blues vocal.

You melt, diaphanous,
and watch red blood cells
navigate your veins.

Mary Milton
"Learn Your Lesson"

the sign read — their idea of a joke —
for the body had been a teacher.
Above the noose her face distorted as though
their ugliness had infiltrated her.

She had spoken out
when silence was their rule.

I walk away from "the lesson."
Snow beneath my feet crunches
like bones of small animals.
My child's arms tighten round my neck
and ensure my silence.

Barbara Minton
You Have to See

You have to see the tree with next year's eyes,
cut just the right amount to let it flow.
The gardener must be extremely wise.

Arms should arch up, a perch for butterflies.
Leave some branches hanging low.
You have to see the tree with next year's eyes.

Trim each dead twig for the space it buys.
It's nine parts art and one part guile, although
the gardener must be extremely wise.

Seal your ears against the tree's sad cries;
try to guess which way the wind will blow.
You have to see the tree with next year's eyes.

Lopping off some buds will certify
a richer, sweeter crop, a neater row.
The gardener must be extremely wise.

By looking forward to a later prize
trees and children both will surely grow.
You have to see them both with next year's eyes.
The gardener must be extremely wise.

Barbara Minton

Baby Teeth

Little chips of Chiclets
on a red velvet bed
in a silver box.
I've carried you
from state to state,
town to town.

Little ivory charms
with tiny bloody
roots, long dried to rust.
Are you still here? I can't
even tell which one belonged to whom.
Every tooth a trauma
in miniature, a chase
around the house, a yank
on a string, an exit in a bite
of red apple.

Why did they resist losing you?
Why did I always have to be the one
who did the pulling?
I'll bury you now, let you
fertilize the philodendron,
and still I wonder how such
tiny things could have left
such big holes.

Barbara Minton
As Far As I Could

I went as far as I could across the desert of your life —
brushed against the cactus of your resentment
felt the thorns of your words.
I traveled miles on the hot sand you strewed
in your wake, sometimes sweeping up after you,
trying to explain to horned toads and diamond-backs
that that was just your way, lashing out at bystanders
with your personal toxins.

I can't count the oases we reached and stayed
a brief moment before you said or did something
and they asked us to leave. Or else, you struck
out on your own, the water soured for you
by its safety and familiarity,
believing it would be better somewhere else,
the people at the next watering hole less stupid
or crazy.

I trekked with you through the jungle of your fear,
battled the twining vines that threatened to strangle
both of us with terror, swatted flies and stinging things
within and without. For you, all the jungle eyes were hostile,
every plant a poison with your name on it. You chopped your way
straight through, and I followed, thinking you knew
what you were doing.

Now I've stopped in a border town, put down
a few straggling roots, but I can still see your form
miles away, plodding on, growing tiny against the sunset.

Barbara Minton
We Fear

We fear
other life forms —
wash Lady Macbeth-wise
to ward off germs,
toss out blue bread
and green cheese,
let no dusty berry
pass our lips,
as though the spores
of our undoing were not
already flowering within us.

Barbara Minton
Prayer in the Schools

At six: please don't let me pee my pants in front of everyone.
At seven: please let me have something good for show and tell.
At eight: let me have a best friend.
At nine: let me have two best friends and don't let them like each other better than me.
At thirteen: when will I get breasts?
At fourteen: please take them back, at least for now.
At fifteen: don't let that boy ask me to the prom.
At sixteen: don't let *that* boy ask me to the prom.
At seventeen: please let *some*one ask me to the prom.
At eighteen: please send a meteor to crash into the prom.

Barbara Minton
Prodigal's Sister

I fed the calf
from a bottle
when her mother
turned her away.

I fed the calf
fresh green shoots
taught her how to forage.

I named the calf
Buttercup after
her favorite blossom.

I wove the calf
a necklace
of clover.

I slept by the calf
when she had colic
gave her medicine.

When he showed up
in rags, smelling
of drink

our father wept
embraced him
gave him cool water.

When he showed up
he had not changed
at all.

When he showed up
our father sent me
to the meadow.

Barbara Minton

Ducklings

Two girls on the grass
one sitting up, the other
lying down, head in her
lover's lap. They are both
shaved bald, and it lends
them a quality of
innocence, like baby ducks.
They don't talk much, only
a word or two — but they
are tender with each other,
and trusting. The sun
glints down on the soft
fuzz that frosts their
round heads.

Barbara Minton
Do-re-mi-fa-sol-la-ti . . .

"tending, as all music does, toward silence . . ."
          Mary Oliver, "When Death Comes"

I've always loved "ti," the seventh
note of the scale. In music theory,
it's called the leading tone
because all it wants, all
it exists for, is to lead
the musical line back home
to "do." It's a powerful note:
it grabs the ear
and pulls — hard —
so hard that we
hear it cross the finish line,
even in modern pieces
written in a language
that has no "do." When I leave the world,
I want to go out
singing the leading tone.

Charles E. Polly

I find
after all these years
I am a believer

I believe Appalachian rain on tin rooftops is the most
haunting sound I have ever heard
I believe the red in ripe strawberries is the most
incredible color
the rainbow has to offer
I believe early morning brewed coffee is the most
invigorating aroma
to ever interrupt my dreams
I believe
the past zips by faster than a roaring river
but not quite fast enough
the future is a device we cook up to save us from ourselves
we mostly succeed
I believe
God is a woman much like my mother and upon her passing
bestowed
a little
everlasting
light
on
me

Charles E. Polly

If Only…

My father were a beaver instead of a snake
>He could have built a dam
>Secure, steady and safe
>Instead of slithering in and out of a Jack Daniels bottle

If only
>My father were a horse instead of a fox
>He could have plowed the fields
>Gardened a home and savored the fruits of his labor
>Instead of masking himself with slyness
>In the weeds of his laziness

If only
>My father were a wolf instead of an owl
>He could have taught us courage
>Instead of raising his hand in anger while hooting words of love
>Instead of throwing away his gifts to the pit of his addiction

If only
>My father were a man
>Strong, wise and confident
>Putting family first over beer, poker and hunting trips

If only
>My father
>>Could have been
>>>More like
>>>>My
>>>>>Mother

Charles E. Polly
mother's hands

were like butterflies on a leash

instead of
asking for a cup of coffee

her hands
would fly from her lap
where they rested

point to the coffee
wave up
dart down
swing from side to side

then

her hands
would flutter
back to her knees
once the cup full of coffee
sat
steaming hot
next to her arm chair

it took me years
to realize
my mother
hated
asking
for
anything

Charles E. Polly

Incident

Once walking 'cross the Golden Gate
No thoughts of any concern
Heavy fog surrounded me
No sun, no fear of burn

Now I am neither short nor tall
My stature unassuming
I had traveled half the bridge
When I felt danger looming

I turned around and saw a man
Who chugged a bottle of beer
He looked at me, stuck out his tongue
And spit out "You're a queer!"

Like a baseball player he wound his arm
And threw the Bud at me
I ducked the pitch and it missed
For drunks can hardly see

I've walked the bridge many a time
And all I can remember
Is the fear and dread I felt
That evening in September.

Charles E. Polly
the view

park bench warm summer day
ducks white on lake
bobbing heads in calm water
birds singing tree tops high
green leaves flowers everywhere
breeze soft
sitting remembering

winter last time here
no summer creature comforts
tears on cheeks frozen stream
much noise mind scattered
loss is cold

mother said life is thin
like ice on creek
too much weight breaks heart

and
mother said be gentle on your path
be strong shoulder heaviness
let pain go with flying birds
      over lake in summer

Charles E. Polly
plagiarist

he was so comfortable
telling his dream to me
delicious purple details
lost in Orinda fog
which enveloped his head
clouded his vision
from familiar trails

his trust genuine
there were no hints
that I
a writer
would lift his dream

exploit his metaphors
make them mine
his languid language
story of weariness

then
guilt set in
much like the fog in his dream
swept over me
wet my muse's fingers
with red ink
leaving a bloody vernacular trail
leading back to him

it made me wonder
simply
by this confession
if
I am
a thief
of my friend's dream

Sue Prince
Dawn

A sighing of morning breeze
shifts a veil of gray-white mist

The eastern sky blushes pink
moss-covered tree trunks pale
accept the present over the past

The morning world bows in silence
vanishes into beams of yellow light
the performance begins.

Sue Prince

The Red String

I.

Many threads entwined
like a litter of newborn pups—
between frayed ends
the string looks solid
feels like chenille
curly soft.

It may have held tightly
the purse strings
of a tender heart
until love, anger, jealousy
loosened the knot
and everything inside
spilled out.

II.

It may have been part of a tangle of fringe
dangling from a once elegant shawl
that draped the shoulders
of a famous chanteuse

as she seductively lounged atop
a polished grand piano
before an enthralled audience.

Long ago, she tossed it
high on a dusty shelf
in a cluttered closet.

Yesterday, she discovered it
dragged it down and
with gnarled fingers
lovingly stroked its faded colors.

One ruddy strand came loose
in the palm of her hand—
She sat wrapped in a wash
of remembrance.

III.

A youth with large, black eyes and chocolate skin
reached down and pulled a single red thread
from the worn carpet.

He crammed it into his pocket
went outside to search
for a flower of the same color

to give to his mother;
He knew a crimson blossom
would make her smile.

Sue Prince

Folds and Unfolds

night folds around day's
warmth, lunar light softens land
cold breeze in canyon

day unfolds into shadow
amber to ebony
owl's delight

waves fold onto beach
foam nibbles sand castle moats
languid expanse

purple desert flowers
unfold where there is nothing
the lizard smiles

hand fold around stem
of crystal wine goblet
a dog barks

chapters unfold page by
page toward conclusion
snails need diet control

the accordion folds
in and out, in and out
everything has its fate

hours unfold whether
desired or despised — time
ultimate hitchhiker

spit-drenched baby fingers
fold around grandma thumb
pie a la mode

Sue Prince

Breakup

I sit in the back of my thinking
drink memory with Beethoven —

images swirl in the wine
mingle with dusky mellow sonatas

and sadness slowly unravels
a once lustrous garment

I sit in the back of my thinking
feel my spirit slide

wordless unspoken
even after dark

in the privacy of rooms
with closed doors.

Joon Stoddart

Did You Ever Meet Somebody Famous?

Did you ever meet somebody famous?
Not for an autograph
or, if asked "Do you want to meet Mr. F.?" I'd say
"Does Mr. F. want to meet me?" Not that.
But did you ever meet somebody famous
just because he was there?

A small photo gallery Greenwich Village
ex-roommate's husband showing his work
plus his friend painter solely of rhinoceri
neither famous not even a little.

Knot of invited viewers surrounded some guy
"It's WeeGee!" they whispered in awe.
He spoke softly, blurred eyes wavering
over the enthralled.
He was short round red-eyed
skin somehow unsavory suspect
I, decked in provincial wonder, stayed.

The rosy eyes rested on me
recognized a girl fresh from the sticks
spoke *sotto voce* of posing for him.
"Bring your mother" he grunted, smirked
reached out a plump claw
touched my breast.

On wings of unspeakable horror
I flew to the far end of the room
where my friends sat doubled in laughter.
"He's at it again."
They were used to the famous.

One friend went off to introduce him
by way of distraction
to a socialite and her limp daughter.

Maybe her mother went with her.

Joon Stoddart
Totem

My chick
my bird
my pet
my downy hatchling
bestowed on me by
my father
I was ten
a hen put to brood
over duck and chicken eggs
alas
when they hatched
flew dementedly against her own
pecked the chicks to death
all but one
rescued by my father.

I named him Bing
as in Crosby
carried him about
on my shoulder
watched in wonder
emerging minute pin feathers
mottled grey
built him a cardboard house
on the front porch
took him out each morning
tucked him in at night.

And so he grew
as did our bond
into a pretty rooster
shining of feather
proud of neck
brilliant of eye.

One day
Mother served him for lunch
fried
I cried
she insisted
"You said it was all right."
no   never   not.

But
that was what our animals
were for
chickens ducks
rabbits turkeys pigs.

And so
I ate the sacrifice
that he
would be
in me.

Joon Stoddart
The
Reason

It's
because
all the time
you're walking
around and wearing
clothes and getting them
dirty and sleeping on sheets
and using towels and they're get-
ting dirty and all that stuff has to be
washed and all the time you're eating
three - four times a day maybe more and
all that stuff has to be bought and cooked and
then cleaned up and all the time the bathroom is
getting dirty and so is the living room and the bed-
rooms and all the other rooms and you have to clean
them and the windows and blinds get dirty and you should
really clean them too and if you have a baby or two or maybe
more they get dirty because they can't help it and they have to be
cleaned and a lot of other stuff like cuddled and curdled and carried
and you have to do that even if you don't do the other stuff and then
if there's someone sick or someone who can't do stuff for themselves
and you have to do that and then there's always the dry cleaning and
holidays and birthdays and trips and stuff like that and then there's
the unexpected stuff like accidents and uninvited company and that's
the part that always gets you, and, well, that's not all by a long shot but
if I could tell you all the stuff I wouldn't have time to do it, and, sure,
if there's only one of you it doesn't seem like much but if there's two
of you it's double and if there're more – well, you get the picture, and
that's the reason why
it's
                    never
                                    done.

Joon Stoddart
Rose of Sharon Home

They sit along the wall
quiet as garden growth
shrunken greyish
so still in this clean space
facing the always television
peaceful as peas

tiny women
small as children
they wait
for families who visit briefly
striving to care

they wait
for the man to come
with the little wriggling dog
that kisses them repeatedly and with passion

they wait
for recurring food
they can no longer taste
eaten together around the oval cherry table

they wait
in their waning season.

Joon Stoddart
Rhythm of Religion

Feel it
unfolding
folding
responding
to the seasons
rising
to the sun
sinking
back
into
the earth
plant
harvest
holy days
holidays
seek food
water
sustenance
light
air
companions
joy
music
resurrection
meaning
of our times
of our life

Joon Stoddart

Message from Maria

Maria Teresa Alvarez
in beautiful flowing script
scratched with a pin
or the tip of a fingernail
on a long green bean

I sat still puzzled
amid supper preparation
mound of fresh beans
to be unstrung
ends clipped steamed eaten

Green bean in my fingers
I thought of a young
Maria Teresa Alvarez
she of the beautiful handwriting

Did she pick this bean
in Salinas fields
or the Imperial Valley
bent over in the punishing sun
long hours long days little pay?

Did she pack beans
in a hot produce barn
sweat sliding longing for hours' end
on her break briefly outside
a cold Coke in the shade
laughing with her friends?

Absently scratched her message:
"Maria Teresa Alvarez
I picked this bean
I packed it
I sent it to you
I
was
here."

Julian Waller
"What, Mr. Beckett,

do you like most about Berlin?"
"I like," he said, "the spaces
between the houses."

The small plot
where the widow tends her roses.

The concrete patch where the man
in the wheelchair rolls out daily
to catch a glimpse of the setting sun.

The thumb-size spot
where a child rides
a tiny trike 'round and 'round,
'round and 'round.

The buffer between the single man
sitting in his parlor,
desperately listening to Beethoven's ninth

and the couple next door
loudly accusing each other
of marital infidelity.

The place where the poet
looks longingly at the sky.

Julian Waller

Closing of Willard State Hospital, Willard, N.Y., 1995

How much dust drifts down
in sixty-five years?
Or eighty-two? Or fifty?
How much dust?

Watered by how many tears?

How much dust did they find
when the attic was cleaned,
the luggage was cleared?
How much dust?

How many tears?

How much grief flew up,
pain poured out
from each opened case
or bag or bundle of clothes,

the pictures, old army uniform,
an airman's wings, a Bible,
that tattered book of names
and addresses, the rosary,
those rings,

the dreams, the hopes...

now scattered on the floor?

Julian Waller
Bleeding

This nation was still in swaddling
when barber-surgeons,
progenitors of my profession,
practiced cupping, purging,
most famously bleeding.
They exsanguinated their way
into the annals of scientific silliness.

But this morning our ancient furnace
declared a holiday. I called
the plumber to mediate.

He descended into Stygian depths.
Rivaling Orpheus, he eventually returned.
I had to bleed the sucker, he said,
and, behold, the furnace,
now well-bled by an expert,
regained its circulation.

Blue toes reverted to pink, no EKGs,
no bypass, no defibrillator-generated
shock therapy, no daring insertion
of stents, no hocus-pocus mumbo-jumbo;
just a good old-fashioned bleed.

Then the need for a second bleed...
and presentation of a non-third party,
non-negotiable bill for services,
the equal of anything members
of my profession would ever think
of charging.

Julian Waller
Waiting

I know you try,
but waiting
is so
damn
long.
Brakes rusted tight,
your body gives in.
You don't.
I won't.
I watch
tar drip
through a sieve,
measuring
eternity,
satisfied
just to be near.

Julian Waller

Time

I always hated that moment
when the proctor, that jack-booted jailor
cadencing the seconds with somber feet,
intoned solemnly, *Five more minutes,* then
Two minutes, finally, desperation
dripping down my face, smiled
and said softly and a bit too gleefully,
Time. Put down your pencils.

It haunts me yet.
In dreams from which I sometimes awake
at three A.M., I am again taking some exam
before which I didn't sleep the night,
didn't study enough, arrived late, and
now my yellow number two Ticonderoga
has turned to sawdust. I watch in horror
as it pours dryly out my nose
and both my ears.

And what of my final moments?
Will some young doctor, stethoscope
draped jauntily over his or her neck
the way I used to let mine poke
just so out of my white intern's
jacket pocket, tell me or my family
I have six months, or three-
two days, perhaps-left to live?

Or will a unisex-black-cloaked Death
sneak up silently behind me
and whisper into my ear, *Put down
your pencil. It's time?*

David White
My Hometown

My hometown is really imaginary —
unless home is where your heart is —
but if it's not, then it's really imaginary —
to me, I mean, not to its current residents,
of course. If your hometown is where you were born,
we moved away when I was two
so I never knew the bus stop on the corner
with that faded fire hydrant and abandoned
galoshes lying on the sidewalk behind the bench.
I was too young to take the bus, my feet too close to my head
to find the floor if I would sit on their green plastic-
covered seats, my arms too short to reach the silver
pull rope to signal the driver to stop
and let me off. So I'd have never gotten off,
I imagine. A two year old forever circling
the city of Cleveland on the bus — eyes just clearing
the lower edge of the metal window frame
and watching, silently, as the city passes by again and again.

David White
Shadow

One of us like a shadow
over water

but it wasn't you —
you were never mere mists of moonlight
flickering on the stillness of a dark lake's surface . . .
no, you were always the very light, itself, to me —
illuminating each letter, each word
my heart would write of you —
but what was written I could never
recite aloud — my voice, useless,
fell silent before the light of you.

No, what my heart wrote, I could not speak.
And what could be spoken never reflected
one part of what you were to me —
what the memory of your quiet beauty
had imprinted on my life —
such treasure; but I, uncomfortable, unwilling miser,
would not, could not, share a penny's worth
of my desire — desire your breath on my cheek
inspired — something glanced but never held —

beauty blunted now by shadow.

David White

Angel's Camp

There's a buzz in the angels' camp —
they've traded harps for accordions.
Each plays a different song . . . a trillion strong —
a hellish cacophony rocks the air.
They stop to think it over . . .

then start again and never stop —
who cares? It may not be celestial
but in heaven, whatever's undertaken
cannot be godforsaken.

David White

Behind Her, Now at the Red Light

and in her car's side view mirror
I see her face: Asian, with lips
small, thin and faded red. Her teeth:
little rounded pearls embedded
in pink-ish gums around which move
those faded lips in carefully

determined patterns — speech? But spent
on whom? Her car: empty, her eyes
vacant but for some dream they see.
Not speech, no, the lips paused and held
a shape too long for mere talk. No,
she sang — to whom? — perhaps her son,
or husband, departed parents
or a friend from days now better
forgotten . . . but not. Her fingers
listless and limp as autumn leaves
rest on the steering wheel's round rim
and like an empty wind no one
feels, her mouth opens and she sings.

David White

The Horse

My hand slides along
the wide expanse of neck
to the shoulder.

The coat is packed tight
with coarse, short hair that grows
flat against its skin —
a kind of flat stubble coating the whole hide
and smooth to the touch if your hand
would glide with the grain of its growth.

Sunny today in the pasture
so my fingers feel that warmth
that the hair now holds.
But I feel something more . . .
not just the heat of late morning . . .
my hand slides along a living thing.
A living thing —
broad, flat muscles washed in innumerable
riverlets of life beneath that hide,
an animating, barely tamed power
far stronger than me or you.

My hand slides along
the wide expanse of neck
and feels a lingering hint of raw animal —
of wildness — not fettered to a yakking intellect
that would cripple access to unmanaged instinct.

Ah, how oddly welcoming to be here
so near so large a being —
this beast with so small a need for humanity.

David White
The Gulls Have Gathered

The gulls have gathered —
their backs against the sky —
to stare at me.

The daylight's grown quiet,
private . . . soft as the evening
stillness when you walk the dogs
by yourself after work.

The older gulls just stare,
the young ones burn with energy:
little jump-flights, wings half open,
to settle back down and stare again, shuffle,
bob their heads, snap their beaks. Communicating
what? I don't know. The old gulls just stare
like retirees sitting in the park surrounded
by the varied crowds walking,
milling aimlessly on sidewalk and grass,
restless with youth.

What do they see as they stare?
Perhaps the unbraiding and unbraiding
of many promises. This will not stop.
Nor is it cause for concern.
To sit is fine. To mill around is fine.

Finally, one of the young gulls
lifts off stretching its wings
against the nothing of air,
heads toward the horizon,
and is gone.

David White

How Delicate

How delicate is the skull.
Maybe not so much when it is filled
with the various moist puddings
and gristle that seem to animate
the collected bits casually
referred to as a 'living being.'

No, not so much then. But later.
When the dust has settled.
When what once filled it
is gone, dried up and carried away
by ant or worm or wind . . .
then the skull, in places, is delicate
almost like paper that careless
fingers can break
and often do.

NOTES

"When I was a cup of tea" was written after using as a prompt Frank Sinatra's song "When I was Seventeen."

"No More Love Sonnets" is a pantoum. In a pantoum, a series of quatrains rhyming *abab* in which the second rhyme of a quatrain recurs as the first in the succeeding quatrain, each quatrain introduces a new second rhyme (as *bcbc, cdcd*), and the initial rhyme of the series recurs as the second rhyme of the closing quatrain (*xaxa*).

"Hummingbird Wings" was inspired by the line "if we knew" by Robert Juarroz. This was used as a prompt in Jannie Dresser's class, Soul Diving.

The prompt, what if you were to write your very last poem about love, inspired "If You Should Die Before Me."

"Planes of View" mentions Algiers, a district of New Orleans only slightly affected by the flooding which followed Hurricane Katrina.

The author explains the context of "Sunday Visit to a Carolina Chain Gang" in the following note. After emancipation, former slaves were arrested on a myriad of petty charges and held on impossibly high bail until some white farmer or plant owner paid their fines and bound them into peonage and perpetual debt.

The author of "You Have to See" gives thanks to David Mas Masumoto for the poem's first line.

The title "I find after all these years I am a believer" is from *ARS POETICA II* by Charles Wright.

"Incident" was inspired by a poem by Counee Cullen, 1925.

The title and first stanza of "What, Mr. Beckett," come from an interview with Samuel Beckett.

Regarding the poem "Closing of Willard State Hospital, Willard, N.Y., 1995," J.P. Strastny and D. Penny in "Lost Luggage, Recovered Lives" (*AJPH* 98:986-988, June, 2008) document the discovery of long abandoned patient luggage and outrageous examples of patient mismanagement when Willard, a mental institution for many decades, was closed in 1995.

ABOUT THE AUTHORS

Rita Flores Bogaert - Writing: breath, sweat of my soul.

Jannie Dresser - Curiosity and generosity: a challenging balance.

Chantal Guillemin - Garden Diary: Planted Seeds. Harvested Poems.

Constance Hester - One of the founding members of Fresh Ink, she has published in numerous journals. Her latest book is *My Name is Myriad.* She currently lives in Albuquerque where she is finishing work on another collection.

Madeline Lacques-Aranda - procrastinates with heart, turning to art

Ellen Levin - watch for the bluebird of happiness

Robin Michel - Birthplace: Utah. Home: Love's Mystery. Grace.

Adam David Miller - The past is not always past.

Mary Milton - Started out good; ending up better.

Barbara Minton - Sang before talking, prosed before poeming.

Charles E. (Chuck) Polly - Chuck Polly: poet; playwright; storyteller; explorer.

Sue Prince - Born and educated on the east coast, she lived poetically for 25 years in Oakland, California and is happily spending her golden years exploring many new activities and making new friends in Paorama in Washington State.

Joon Stoddart - Keep moving   Keep dreaming   Keep laughing

Julian Waller - Writing poetry since 1994 upon completing a career as a public health physician and Professor of Medicine at the University of Vermont, he recently returned to Vermont, after thirteen years in the Bay Area, where he continues both his poetic and artistic activities.

David White - Suns have light as do hearts.

CPSIA information can be obtained at www.ICGtesting.com
Printed in the USA
BVOW041611211111

276634BV00001B/89/P